BICHON FRISE

browntrout publishers, inc.

www.browntrout.com

AUSTRALIA & NEW ZEALAND

BrownTrout Publishers Pty. Ltd.
12 Mareno Road
Tullamarine VIC 3043, Australia
03 9338 4766
Outside Australia: (61) 3 9338 4766
Australia Toll Free: 1 800 111 882
New Zealand Toll Free: 0800 888 112
sales@browntrout.com.au

UNITED KINGDOM

BrownTrout Publishers Ltd.
P.O. Box 201
Bristol BS99 5ZE England UK
(44) 117 317 1880
UK Freephone: 0800 169 3718
sales@browntroutuk.com

CANADA

BrownTrout Publishers Ltd.
55 Cork Street East, Unit 206
Guelph ON N1H 2W7, Canada
(1) 519 821 8882
Canada Toll Free: 1 888 254 5842
Fax: (1) 519 821 1012
sales@browntrout.ca

MEXICO

Editorial SalmoTruti, SA de CV
Hegel 153 Int. 903, Colonia Polanco,
Del. Miguel Hidalgo, 11560 Mexico D.F.,
Mexico
(52-55) 5545 0492
Mexico Toll Free: 01 800 716 7420
ventas@salmotruti.com.mx

2011 YEAR PLANNER

JANUARY	FEBRUARY	MARCH	APRIL
1 SAT	1 TUE	1 TUE	1 FRI
2 SUN	2 WED	2 WED	2 SAT
3 MON	3 THU	3 THU	3 SUN
4 TUE	4 FRI	4 FRI	4 MON
5 WED	5 SAT	5 SAT	5 TUE
6 THU	6 SUN	6 SUN	6 WED
7 FRI	7 MON	7 MON	7 THU
8 SAT	8 TUE	8 TUE	8 FRI
9 SUN	9 WED	9 WED	9 SAT
10 MON	10 THU	10 THU	10 SUN
11 TUE	11 FRI	11 FRI	11 MON
12 WED	12 SAT	12 SAT	12 TUE
13 THU	13 SUN	13 SUN	13 WED
14 FRI	14 MON	14 MON	14 THU
15 SAT	15 TUE	15 TUE	15 FRI
16 SUN	16 WED	16 WED	16 SAT
17 MON	17 THU	17 THU	17 SUN
18 TUE	18 FRI	18 FRI	18 MON
19 WED	19 SAT	19 SAT	19 TUE
20 THU	20 SUN	20 SUN	20 WED
21 FRI	21 MON	21 MON	21 THU
22 SAT	22 TUE	22 TUE	22 FRI
23 SUN	23 WED	23 WED	23 SAT
24 MON	24 THU	24 THU	24 SUN
25 TUE	25 FRI	25 FRI	25 MON
26 WED	26 SAT	26 SAT	26 TUE
27 THU	27 SUN	27 SUN	27 WED
28 FRI	28 MON	28 MON	28 THU
29 SAT		29 TUE	29 FRI
30 SUN		30 WED	30 SAT
31 MON		31 THU	

2011 YEAR PLANNER

MAY	JUNE	JULY	AUGUST
1 **SUN**	1 WED	1 FRI	1 MON
2 MON	2 THU	2 **SAT**	2 TUE
3 TUE	3 FRI	3 **SUN**	3 WED
4 WED	4 **SAT**	4 MON	4 THU
5 THU	5 **SUN**	5 TUE	5 FRI
6 FRI	6 MON	6 WED	6 **SAT**
7 **SAT**	7 TUE	7 THU	7 **SUN**
8 **SUN**	8 WED	8 FRI	8 MON
9 MON	9 THU	9 **SAT**	9 TUE
10 TUE	10 FRI	10 **SUN**	10 WED
11 WED	11 **SAT**	11 MON	11 THU
12 THU	12 **SUN**	12 TUE	12 FRI
13 FRI	13 MON	13 WED	13 **SAT**
14 **SAT**	14 TUE	14 THU	14 **SUN**
15 **SUN**	15 WED	15 FRI	15 MON
16 MON	16 THU	16 **SAT**	16 TUE
17 TUE	17 FRI	17 **SUN**	17 WED
18 WED	18 **SAT**	18 MON	18 THU
19 THU	19 **SUN**	19 TUE	19 FRI
20 FRI	20 MON	20 WED	20 **SAT**
21 **SAT**	21 TUE	21 THU	21 **SUN**
22 **SUN**	22 WED	22 FRI	22 MON
23 MON	23 THU	23 **SAT**	23 TUE
24 TUE	24 FRI	24 **SUN**	24 WED
25 WED	25 **SAT**	25 MON	25 THU
26 THU	26 **SUN**	26 TUE	26 FRI
27 FRI	27 MON	27 WED	27 **SAT**
28 **SAT**	28 TUE	28 THU	28 **SUN**
29 **SUN**	29 WED	29 FRI	29 MON
30 MON	30 THU	30 **SAT**	30 TUE
31 TUE		31 **SUN**	31 WED

2011 YEAR PLANNER

SEPTEMBER	OCTOBER	NOVEMBER	DECEMBER
1 THU	1 SAT	1 TUE	1 THU
2 FRI	2 SUN	2 WED	2 FRI
3 SAT	3 MON	3 THU	3 SAT
4 SUN	4 TUE	4 FRI	4 SUN
5 MON	5 WED	5 SAT	5 MON
6 TUE	6 THU	6 SUN	6 TUE
7 WED	7 FRI	7 MON	7 WED
8 THU	8 SAT	8 TUE	8 THU
9 FRI	9 SUN	9 WED	9 FRI
10 SAT	10 MON	10 THU	10 SAT
11 SUN	11 TUE	11 FRI	11 SUN
12 MON	12 WED	12 SAT	12 MON
13 TUE	13 THU	13 SUN	13 TUE
14 WED	14 FRI	14 MON	14 WED
15 THU	15 SAT	15 TUE	15 THU
16 FRI	16 SUN	16 WED	16 FRI
17 SAT	17 MON	17 THU	17 SAT
18 SUN	18 TUE	18 FRI	18 SUN
19 MON	19 WED	19 SAT	19 MON
20 TUE	20 THU	20 SUN	20 TUE
21 WED	21 FRI	21 MON	21 WED
22 THU	22 SAT	22 TUE	22 THU
23 FRI	23 SUN	23 WED	23 FRI
24 SAT	24 MON	24 THU	24 SAT
25 SUN	25 TUE	25 FRI	25 SUN
26 MON	26 WED	26 SAT	26 MON
27 TUE	27 THU	27 SUN	27 TUE
28 WED	28 FRI	28 MON	28 WED
29 THU	29 SAT	29 TUE	29 THU
30 FRI	30 SUN	30 WED	30 FRI
	31 MON		31 SAT

26
SUN
DIM.DOM.SON

27
MON
LUN.LUN.MON

Last Quarter ◑ 4:18 U.T

28
TUE
MAR.MAR.DIE

29
WED
MER.MIÉR.MIT

30
THU
JEU.JUE.DON

31
FRI
VEN.VIER.FRE

JANUARY 2011

1
SAT
SAM.SÁB.SAM

Kwanzaa ends

New Year's Day   Jour de l'An   Año Nuevo

	S	S	M	T	W	TH	F	S	S	M	T	W	TH	F	S	S	M	T	W	TH	F	S	S	M	T	W	TH	F
DECEMBER 2010					1	2	3	**4**	**5**	6	7	8	9	10	**11**	**12**	13	14	15	16	17	**18**	**19**	20	21	22	23	24
JANUARY 2011	**1**	**2**	3	4	5	6	7	**8**	**9**	10	11	12	13	14	**15**	**16**	17	18	19	20	21	**22**	**23**	24	25	26	27	28
FEBRUARY 2011			1	2	3	4	**5**	**6**	7	8	9	10	11	**12**	**13**	14	15	16	17	18	**19**	**20**	21	22	23	24	25	**26**

2
SUN
DIM.DOM.SON

Perihelion 19:00 U.T.

3
MON
LUN.LUN.MON

Bank Holiday (UK)

Day after New Year's Day (NZ)

New Moon ● 9:03 U.T. / Solar Eclipse (Partial) 8:51 U.T.

4
TUE
MAR.MAR.DIE

Bank Holiday (SCT)

5
WED
MER.MIÉR.MIT

6
THU
JEU.JUE.DON

Epiphany   Épiphanie   Día de los Reyes

7
FRI
VEN.VIER.FRE

8
SAT
SAM.SÁB.SAM

	S	S	M	T	W	TH	F	S	S	M	T	W	TH	F	S	S	M	T	W	TH	F	S	S	M	T	W	TH	F	S	S	M	T	W	TH	F
DECEMBER 2010					1	2	3	**4**	**5**	6	7	8	9	10	**11**	**12**	13	14	15	16	17	**18**	**19**	20	21	22	23	24	**25**	**26**	27	28	29	30	31
JANUARY 2011	**1**	**2**	3	4	5	6	7	**8**	**9**	10	11	12	13	14	**15**	**16**	17	18	19	20	21	**22**	**23**	24	25	26	27	28	**29**	**30**	31				
FEBRUARY 2011				1	2	3	4	**5**	**6**	7	8	9	10	11	**12**	**13**	14	15	16	17	18	**19**	**20**	21	22	23	24	25	**26**	**27**	28				

9
SUN
DIM.DOM.SON

10
MON
LUN.LUN.MON

11
TUE
MAR.MAR.DIE

First Quarter ◗ 11:31 U.T.

12
WED
MER.MIÉR.MIT

13
THU
JEU.JUE.DON

14
FRI
VEN.VIER.FRE

15
SAT
SAM.SÁB.SAM

	S	S	M	T	W	TH	F	S	S	M	T	W	TH	F	S	S	M	T	W	TH	F	S	S	M	T	W	TH	F
DECEMBER 2010					1	2	3	**4**	**5**	6	7	8	9	10	**11**	**12**	13	14	15	16	17	**18**	**19**	20	21	22	23	24	**25**	**26**	27	28	29	30	31
JANUARY 2011	**1**	**2**	3	4	5	6	7	**8**	**9**	10	11	12	13	14	**15**	**16**	17	18	19	20	21	**22**	**23**	24	25	26	27	28	**29**	**30**	31
FEBRUARY 2011			1	2	3	4	**5**	**6**	7	8	9	10	11	**12**	**13**	14	15	16	17	18	**19**	**20**	21	22	23	24	25	**26**	**27**	28

16
SUN
DIM.DOM.SON

17
MON
LUN.LUN.MON

Rev. Martin Luther King, Jr. Day (US)

18
TUE
MAR.MAR.DIE

Full Moon ◯ 21:21 U.T.

19
WED
MER.MIÉR.MIT

20
THU
JEU.JUE.DON

21
FRI
VEN.VIER.FRE

22
SAT
SAM.SÁB.SAM

	S	S	M	T	W	TH	F	S	S	M	T	W	TH	F	S	S	M	T	W	TH	F	S	S	M	T	W	TH	F	S	S	M	T	W	TH	F
DECEMBER 2010					1	2	3	**4**	**5**	6	7	8	9	10	**11**	**12**	13	14	15	16	17	**18**	**19**	20	21	22	23	24	**25**	**26**	27	28	29	30	31
JANUARY 2011	**1**	**2**	3	4	5	6	7	**8**	**9**	10	11	12	13	14	**15**	**16**	17	18	19	20	21	**22**	**23**	24	25	26	27	28	**29**	**30**	31				
FEBRUARY 2011			1	2	3	4	**5**	**6**	7	8	9	10	11	**12**	**13**	14	15	16	17	18	**19**	**20**	21	22	23	24	25	**26**	**27**	28					

23
SUN
DIM.DOM.SON

24
MON
LUN.LUN.MON

25
TUE
MAR.MAR.DIE

Burns Night (SCT

Last Quarter ◑ 12:57 U.T

26
WED
MER.MIÉR.MIT

Australia Day (AU

27
THU
JEU.JUE.DON

Holocaust Memorial Day (UN

28
FRI
VEN.VIER.FRE

29
SAT
SAM.SÁB.SAM

	S	S	M	T	W	TH	F	S	S	M	T	W	TH	F	S	S	M	T	W	TH	F	S	S	M	T	W	TH	F	S	S	M	T	W	TH	F
DECEMBER 2010					1	2	3	**4**	**5**	6	7	8	9	10	**11**	**12**	13	14	15	16	17	**18**	**19**	20	21	22	23	24	**25**	**26**	27	28	29	30	31
JANUARY 2011	**1**	**2**	3	4	5	6	7	**8**	**9**	10	11	12	13	14	**15**	**16**	17	18	19	20	21	**22**	**23**	24	25	26	27	28	**29**	**30**	31				
FEBRUARY 2011				1	2	3	4	**5**	**6**	7	8	9	10	11	**12**	**13**	14	15	16	17	18	**19**	**20**	21	22	23	24	25	**26**	**27**	28				

30
SUN
DIM.DOM.SON

31
MON
LUN.LUN.MON

FEBRUARY 2011

1
TUE
MAR.MAR.DIE

2
WED
MER.MIÉR.MIT

Groundhog Day

Día de la Candelaria (MX)

New Moon ● 2:31 U.T.

3
THU
JEU.JUE.DON

Chinese New Year– Year of the Rabbit

4
FRI
VEN.VIER.FRE

5
SAT
SAM.SÁB.SAM

Día de la Constitución (MX)

	S	S	M	T	W	TH	F	S	S	M	T	W	TH	F	S	S	M	T	W	TH	F	S	S	M	T	W	TH	F	S	S	M	T	W	TH	F
JANUARY 2011	1	2	3	4	5	6	7	8	9	10	11	12	13	14	15	16	17	18	19	20	21	22	23	24	25	26	27	28	29	30	31				
FEBRUARY 2011			1	2	3	4	5	6	7	8	9	10	11	12	13	14	15	16	17	18	19	20	21	22	23	24	25	26	27	28					
MARCH 2011			1	2	3	4	5	6	7	8	9	10	11	12	13	14	15	16	17	18	19	20	21	22	23	24	25	26	27	28	29	30	31		

6
SUN
DIM.DOM.SON

Waitangi Day (N

7
MON
LUN.LUN.MON

8
TUE
MAR.MAR.DIE

9
WED
MER.MIÉR.MIT

10
THU
JEU.JUE.DON

First Quarter ◑ 7:18 U

11
FRI
VEN.VIER.FRE

12
SAT
SAM.SÁB.SAM

Lincoln's Birthday (U

	S	S	M	T	W	TH	F	S	S	M	T	W	TH	F	S	S	M	T	W	TH	F	S	S	M	T	W	TH	F	S	S	M	T	W	TH	F
JANUARY 2011	1	2	3	4	5	6	7	8	9	10	11	12	13	14	15	16	17	18	19	20	21	22	23	24	25	26	27	28	29	30	31				
FEBRUARY 2011				1	2	3	4	5	6	7	8	9	10	11	12	13	14	15	16	17	18	19	20	21	22	23	24	25	26	27	28				
MARCH 2011				1	2	3	4	5	6	7	8	9	10	11	12	13	14	15	16	17	18	19	20	21	22	23	24	25	26	27	28	29	30	31	

13
SUN
DIM.DOM.SON

14
MON
LUN.LUN.MON

Valentine's Day   Saint-Valentin

Día del Amor y la Amistad (MX)

15
TUE
MAR.MAR.DIE

16
WED
MER.MIÉR.MIT

17
THU
JEU.JUE.DON

Full Moon ◯ 8:36 U.T.

18
FRI
VEN.VIER.FRE

19
SAT
SAM.SÁB.SAM

	S	S	M	T	W	TH	F	S	S	M	T	W	TH	F	S	S	M	T	W	TH	F	S	S	M	T	W	TH	F
JANUARY 2011	**1**	**2**	3	4	5	6	7	**8**	**9**	10	11	12	13	14	**15**	**16**	17	18	19	20	21	**22**	**23**	24	25	26	27	28	**29**	**30**	31
FEBRUARY 2011			1	2	3	4	**5**	**6**	7	8	9	10	11	**12**	**13**	14	15	16	17	18	**19**	**20**	21	22	23	24	25	**26**	**27**	28
MARCH 2011			1	2	3	4	**5**	**6**	7	8	9	10	11	**12**	**13**	14	15	16	17	18	**19**	**20**	21	22	23	24	25	**26**	**27**	28	29	30	31

20
SUN
DIM.DOM.SON

21
MON
LUN.LUN.MON

Presidents' Day (US)

Family Day (AB, ON, SK - CAN)

22
TUE
MAR.MAR.DIE

Washington's Birthday (US)

23
WED
MER.MIÉR.MIT

24
THU
JEU.JUE.DON

Last Quarter ◗ 23:26 U.T.

Día de la Bandera (MX)

25
FRI
VEN.VIER.FRE

26
SAT
SAM.SÁB.SAM

	S	S	M	T	W	TH	F	S	S	M	T	W	TH	F	S	S	M	T	W	TH	F	S	S	M	T	W	TH	F	S	S	M	T	W	TH	F
JANUARY 2011	1	2	3	4	5	6	7	8	9	10	11	12	13	14	15	16	17	18	19	20	21	22	23	24	25	26	27	28	29	30	31				
FEBRUARY 2011				1	2	3	4	5	6	7	8	9	10	11	12	13	14	15	16	17	18	19	20	21	22	23	24	25	26	27	28				
MARCH 2011				1	2	3	4	5	6	7	8	9	10	11	12	13	14	15	16	17	18	19	20	21	22	23	24	25	26	27	28	29	30	31	

27
SUN
DIM.DOM.SON

28
MON
LUN.LUN.MON

MARCH2011

1
TUE
MAR.MAR.DIE

St. David's Day (WAL)

2
WED
MER.MIÉR.MIT

3
THU
JEU.JUE.DON

New Moon ● 20:46 U.T.

4
FRI
VEN.VIER.FRE

5
SAT
SAM.SÁB.SAM

	F	S	S	M	T	W	TH	F	S	S	M	T	W	TH	F	S	S	M	T	W	TH	F	S	S	M	T	W	TH	F	S	S	M	T	W	TH
FEBRUARY 2011					1	2	3	4	**5**	**6**	7	8	9	10	11	**12**	**13**	14	15	16	17	18	**19**	**20**	21	22	23	24	25	**26**	**27**	28			
MARCH 2011					1	2	3	4	**5**	**6**	7	8	9	10	11	**12**	**13**	14	15	16	17	18	**19**	**20**	21	22	23	24	25	**26**	**27**	28	29	30	31
APRIL 2011	1	**2**	**3**	4	5	6	7	8	**9**	**10**	11	12	13	14	15	**16**	**17**	18	19	20	21	22	**23**	**24**	25	26	27	28	29	**30**					

6
SUN
DIM.DOM.SON

7
MON
LUN.LUN.MON

Labour Day (WA - AU)

Great Lent begins (Orthodox)

8
TUE
MAR.MAR.DIE

Shrove Tuesday

Fat Tuesday   Mardi gras   Martes de Carnaval

International Women's Day

9
WED
MER.MIÉR.MIT

Ash Wednesday   Mercredi des Cendres   Miércoles de Ceniza

10
THU
JEU.JUE.DON

11
FRI
VEN.VIER.FRE

First Quarter ◐ 23:45 U.T.

12
SAT
SAM.SÄB.SAM

	F	S	S	M	T	W	TH	F	S	S	M	T	W	TH	F	S	S	M	T	W	TH	F	S	S	M	T	W	TH
FEBRUARY 2011					1	2	3	4	5	6	7	8	9	10	11	12	13	14	15	16	17	18	19	20	21	22	23	24	25	26	27	28
MARCH 2011					1	2	3	4	5	6	7	8	9	10	11	12	13	14	15	16	17	18	19	20	21	22	23	24	25	26	27	28	29	30	31
APRIL 2011	1	2	3	4	5	6	7	8	9	10	11	12	13	14	15	16	17	18	19	20	21	22	23	24	25	26	27	28	29	30

13
SUN
DIM.DOM.SON

Daylight Saving Time begins (US; CAN)

14
MON
LUN.LUN.MON

Commonwealth Day

Labour Day (VIC - AU)

Eight Hours Day (TAS - AU)

15
TUE
MAR.MAR.DIE

16
WED
MER.MIÉR.MIT

17
THU
JEU.JUE.DON

St. Patrick's Day   Saint-Patrick   San Patricio

18
FRI
VEN.VIER.FRE

Full Moon ○ 18:10 U.T.

19
SAT
SAM.SÁB.SAM

	F	S	S	M	T	W	TH	F	S	S	M	T	W	TH	F	S	S	M	T	W	TH	F	S	S	M	T	W	TH	F	S	S	M	T	W	TH
FEBRUARY 2011					1	2	3	4	5	6	7	8	9	10	11	12	13	14	15	16	17	18	19	20	21	22	23	24	25	26	27	28			
MARCH 2011					1	2	3	4	5	6	7	8	9	10	11	12	13	14	15	16	17	18	19	20	21	22	23	24	25	26	27	28	29	30	31
APRIL 2011	1	2	3	4	5	6	7	8	9	10	11	12	13	14	15	16	17	18	19	20	21	22	23	24	25	26	27	28	29	30					

Vernal Equinox 23:21 U.T

20
SUN
DIM.DOM.SON

Journée internationale de la Francophonie   Int'l Speakers of French Day

21
MON
LUN.LUN.MON

Natalicio de Benito Juárez (MX

22
TUE
MAR.MAR.DIE

23
WED
MER.MIÉR.MIT

24
THU
JEU.JUE.DON

25
FRI
VEN.VIER.FRE

Last Quarter  12:07 U.T

26
SAT
SAM.SÁB.SAM

	F	S	S	M	T	W	TH	F	S	S	M	T	W	TH	F	S	S	M	T	W	TH	F	S	S	M	T	W	TH	F	S	S	M	T	W	TH
FEBRUARY 2011					1	2	3	4	5	6	7	8	9	10	11	12	13	14	15	16	17	18	19	20	21	22	23	24	25	26	27	28			
MARCH 2011					1	2	3	4	5	6	7	8	9	10	11	12	13	14	15	16	17	18	19	20	21	22	23	24	25	26	27	28	29	30	31
APRIL 2011	1	2	3	4	5	6	7	8	9	10	11	12	13	14	15	16	17	18	19	20	21	22	23	24	25	26	27	28	29	30					

27
SUN
DIM.DOM.SON

European Union Daylight Saving Time begins

28
MON
LUN.LUN.MON

29
TUE
MAR.MAR.DIE

30
WED
MER.MIÉR.MIT

31
THU
JEU.JUE.DON

APRIL 2011

1
FRI
VEN.VIER.FRE

April Fools' Day

2
SAT
SAM.SÁB.SAM

	F	S	S	M	T	W	TH	F	S	S	M	T	W	TH	F	S	S	M	T	W	TH	F	S	S	M	T	W	TH
FEBRUARY 2011				1	2	3	4	5	6	7	8	9	10	11	12	13	14	15	16	17	18	19	20	21	22	23	24	25	26	27	28
MARCH 2011				1	2	3	4	5	6	7	8	9	10	11	12	13	14	15	16	17	18	19	20	21	22	23	24	25	26	27	28	29	30	31
APRIL 2011	1	2	3	4	5	6	7	8	9	10	11	12	13	14	15	16	17	18	19	20	21	22	23	24	25	26	27	28	29	30

New Moon ● 14:32 U

3
SUN
DIM.DOM.SON

Mothering Sunday (U

Daylight Saving Time ends (N

4
MON
LUN.LUN.MON

5
TUE
MAR.MAR.DIE

6
WED
MER.MIÉR.MIT

7
THU
JEU.JUE.DON

8
FRI
VEN.VIER.FRE

9
SAT
SAM.SÁB.SAM

	F	S	S	M	T	W	TH	F	S	S	M	T	W	TH	F	S	S	M	T	W	TH	F	S	S	M	T	W	TH
MARCH 2011					1	2	3	4	5	6	7	8	9	10	11	12	13	14	15	16	17	18	19	20	21	22	23	24	25	26	27	28	29	30	31
APRIL 2011	1	2	3	4	5	6	7	8	9	10	11	12	13	14	15	16	17	18	19	20	21	22	23	24	25	26	27	28	29	30
MAY 2011		1	2	3	4	5	6	7	8	9	10	11	12	13	14	15	16	17	18	19	20	21	22	23	24	25	26	27	28	29	30	31

10
SUN
DIM.DOM.SON

First Quarter  12:05 U.T.

11
MON
LUN.LUN.MON

12
TUE
MAR.MAR.DIE

13
WED
MER.MIÉR.MIT

14
THU
JEU.JUE.DON

15
FRI
VEN.VIER.FRE

16
SAT
SAM.SÁB.SAM

	F	**S**	**S**	M	T	W	TH	F	**S**	**S**	M	T	W	TH	F	**S**	**S**	M	T	W	TH	F	**S**	**S**	M	T	W	TH	F	**S**	**S**	M	T	W	TH
MARCH 2011					1	2	3	4	**5**	**6**	7	8	9	10	11	**12**	**13**	14	15	16	17	18	**19**	**20**	21	22	23	24	25	**26**	**27**	28	29	30	31
APRIL 2011	1	**2**	**3**	4	5	6	7	8	**9**	**10**	11	12	13	14	15	**16**	**17**	18	19	20	21	22	**23**	**24**	25	26	27	28	29	**30**					
MAY 2011		**1**	2	3	4	5	6	7	**8**	**9**	10	11	12	13	14	**15**	**16**	17	18	19	20	21	**22**	**23**	24	25	26	27	28	**29**	**30**	31			

17
SUN
DIM.DOM.SON

Palm Sunday   Dimanche des Rameaux   Domingo de Ramos

Full Moon ○ 2:44 U.T.

18
MON
LUN.LUN.MON

Passover begins at sundown

19
TUE
MAR.MAR.DIE

20
WED
MER.MIÉR.MIT

21
THU
JEU.JUE.DON

Birthday of Queen Elizabeth II

Maundy Thursday   Jeudi saint   Jueves Santo

22
FRI
VEN.VIER.FRE

Earth Day

Bank Holiday (UK)

Good Friday   Vendredi saint   Viernes Santo

23
SAT
SAM.SÁB.SAM

St. George's Day (ENG)

Holy Saturday   Samedi saint   Sábado de Gloria

	F	S	S	M	T	W	TH	F	S	S	M	T	W	TH	F	S	S	M	T	W	TH	F	S	S	M	T	W	TH
MARCH 2011					1	2	3	4	**5**	**6**	7	8	9	10	11	**12**	**13**	14	15	16	17	18	**19**	**20**	21	22	23	24	25	**26**	**27**	28	29	30	31
APRIL 2011	1	**2**	**3**	4	5	6	7	8	**9**	**10**	11	12	13	14	15	**16**	**17**	18	19	20	21	22	**23**	**24**	25	26	27	28	29	**30**
MAY 2011		**1**	2	3	4	5	6	**7**	**8**	9	10	11	12	13	**14**	**15**	16	17	18	19	20	**21**	**22**	23	24	25	26	27	**28**	**29**	30	31

Pascha (Orthodox)

Easter Sunday   Pâques   Domingo de Pascua

Last Quarter 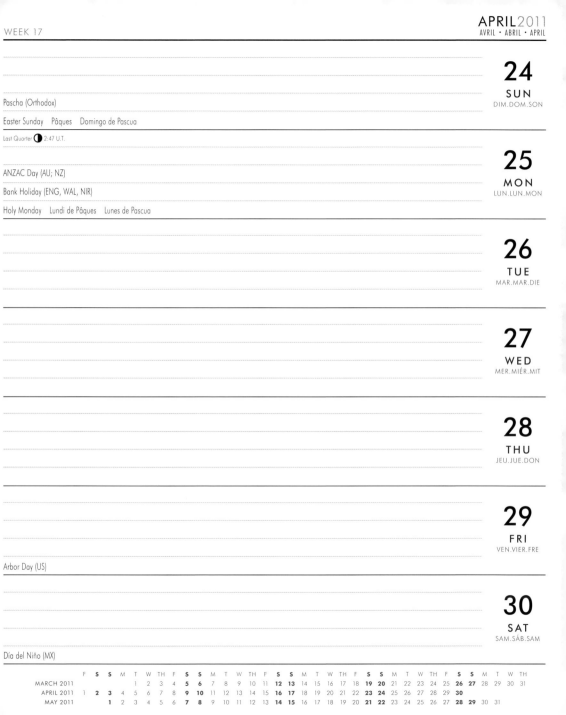 2:47 U.T.

24
SUN
DIM.DOM.SON

ANZAC Day (AU; NZ)

Bank Holiday (ENG, WAL, NIR)

Holy Monday   Lundi de Pâques   Lunes de Pascua

25
MON
LUN.LUN.MON

26
TUE
MAR.MAR.DIE

27
WED
MER.MIÉR.MIT

28
THU
JEU.JUE.DON

Arbor Day (US)

29
FRI
VEN.VIER.FRE

Día del Niño (MX)

30
SAT
SAM.SÁB.SAM

	F	S	S	M	T	W	TH	F	S	S	M	T	W	TH	F	S	S	M	T	W	TH	F	S	S	M	T	W	TH
MARCH 2011					1	2	3	4	**5**	**6**	7	8	9	10	11	**12**	**13**	14	15	16	17	18	**19**	**20**	21	22	23	24	25	**26**	**27**	28	29	30	31
APRIL 2011	1	**2**	**3**	4	5	6	7	8	**9**	**10**	11	12	13	14	15	**16**	**17**	18	19	20	21	22	**23**	**24**	25	26	27	28	29	**30**
MAY 2011		**1**	2	3	4	5	6	**7**	**8**	9	10	11	12	13	**14**	**15**	16	17	18	19	20	**21**	**22**	23	24	25	26	27	**28**	**29**	30	31

1
SUN
DIM.DOM.SON

National Pet Week (US)

May Day

International Workers' Day   Fête du Travail (FR)   Día del Trabajo (MX)

2
MON
LUN.LUN.MON

May Day (NT - AU)

Labour Day (QLD - AU)

Early May Bank Holiday (UK)

New Moon ● 6:51 U.T.

3
TUE
MAR.MAR.DIE

4
WED
MER.MIÉR.MIT

5
THU
JEU.JUE.DON

Batalla de Puebla (MX)

6
FRI
VEN.VIER.FRE

7
SAT
SAM.SÁB.SAM

	F	S	S	M	T	W	TH	F	S	S	M	T	W	TH	F	S	S	M	T	W	TH	F	S	S	M	T	W	TH	F	S	S	M	T	W	TH
APRIL 2011	1	**2**	**3**	4	5	6	7	8	**9**	**10**	11	12	13	14	15	**16**	**17**	18	19	20	21	22	**23**	**24**	25	26	27	28	29	**30**					
MAY 2011			**1**	2	3	4	5	6	**7**	**8**	9	10	11	12	13	**14**	**15**	16	17	18	19	20	**21**	**22**	23	24	25	26	27	**28**	**29**	30	31		
JUNE 2011				1	2	3	**4**	**5**	6	7	8	9	10	**11**	**12**	13	14	15	16	17	**18**	**19**	20	21	22	23	24	**25**	**26**	27	28	29	30		

Mother's Day (US; AU; CAN; NZ)
Fête des Mères (CAN)
Fête de la Victoire (FR)

8
SUN
DIM.DOM.SON

9
MON
LUN.LUN.MON

First Quarter ◐ 20:33 U.T.

10
TUE
MAR.MAR.DIE

Día de las Madres (MX)

11
WED
MER.MIÉR.MIT

12
THU
JEU.JUE.DON

13
FRI
VEN.VIER.FRE

14
SAT
SAM.SÁB.SAM

	F	**S**	**S**	M	T	W	TH	F	**S**	**S**	M	T	W	TH	F	**S**	**S**	M	T	W	TH	F	**S**	**S**	M	T	W	TH	F	**S**	**S**	M	T	W	TH
APRIL 2011	1	**2**	**3**	4	5	6	7	8	**9**	**10**	11	12	13	14	15	**16**	**17**	18	19	20	21	22	**23**	**24**	25	26	27	28	29	**30**					
MAY 2011			**1**	2	3	4	5	6	**7**	**8**	9	10	11	12	13	**14**	**15**	16	17	18	19	20	**21**	**22**	23	24	25	26	27	**28**	**29**	30	31		
JUNE 2011						1	2	3	**4**	**5**	6	7	8	9	10	**11**	**12**	13	14	15	16	17	**18**	**19**	20	21	22	23	24	**25**	**26**	27	28	29	30

15
SUN
DIM.DOM.SON

Día del Maestro (MX

16
MON
LUN.LUN.MON

Full Moon ○ 11:09 U.

17
TUE
MAR.MAR.DIE

18
WED
MER.MIÉR.MIT

19
THU
JEU.JUE.DON

20
FRI
VEN.VIER.FRE

21
SAT
SAM.SÁB.SAM

	F	S	S	M	T	W	TH	F	S	S	M	T	W	TH	F	S	S	M	T	W	TH	F	S	S	M	T	W	TH	F	S	S	M	T	W	TH
APRIL 2011	1	2	3	4	5	6	7	8	9	10	11	12	13	14	15	16	17	18	19	20	21	22	23	24	25	26	27	28	29	30					
MAY 2011		1	2	3	4	5	6	7	8	9	10	11	12	13	14	15	16	17	18	19	20	21	22	23	24	25	26	27	28	29	30	31			
JUNE 2011					1	2	3	4	5	6	7	8	9	10	11	12	13	14	15	16	17	18	19	20	21	22	23	24	25	26	27	28	29	30	

22
SUN
DIM.DOM.SON

23
MON
LUN.LUN.MON

Victoria Day (CAN)

La Journée nationale des patriotes (QC - CAN)

Last Quarter 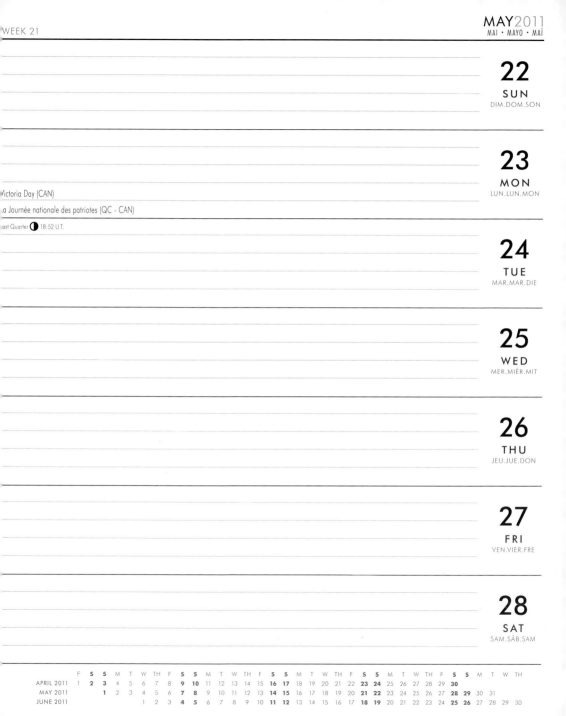 18:52 U.T.

24
TUE
MAR.MAR.DIE

25
WED
MER.MIÉR.MIT

26
THU
JEU.JUE.DON

27
FRI
VEN.VIER.FRE

28
SAT
SAM.SÁB.SAM

	F	S	S	M	T	W	TH	F	S	S	M	T	W	TH	F	S	S	M	T	W	TH	F	S	S	M	T	W	TH
APRIL 2011	1	2	3	4	5	6	7	8	9	10	11	12	13	14	15	16	17	18	19	20	21	22	23	24	25	26	27	28	29	30
MAY 2011		1	2	3	4	5	6	7	8	9	10	11	12	13	14	15	16	17	18	19	20	21	22	23	24	25	26	27	28	29	30	31
JUNE 2011					1	2	3	4	5	6	7	8	9	10	11	12	13	14	15	16	17	18	19	20	21	22	23	24	25	26	27	28	29	30

29
SUN
DIM.DOM.SON

Fête des Mères (FR

30
MON
LUN.LUN.MON

Memorial Day (US

Spring Bank Holiday (UK

31
TUE
MAR.MAR.DIE

JUNE2011

New Moon ● 21:03 U.T. / Solar Eclipse (Partial) 21:17 U.T

1
WED
MER.MIÉR.MIT

2
THU
JEU.JUE.DON

3
FRI
VEN.VIER.FRE

4
SAT
SAM.SÁB.SAM

	F	S	S	M	T	W	TH	F	S	S	M	T	W	TH	F	S	S	M	T	W	TH	F	S	S	M	T	W	TH	F	S	S	M	T	W	TH
APRIL 2011	1	**2**	**3**	4	5	6	7	8	**9**	**10**	11	12	13	14	15	**16**	**17**	18	19	20	21	22	**23**	**24**	25	26	27	28	29	**30**					
MAY 2011			**1**	2	3	4	5	6	**7**	**8**	9	10	11	12	13	**14**	**15**	16	17	18	19	20	**21**	**22**	23	24	25	26	27	**28**	**29**	30	31		
JUNE 2011						1	2	3	**4**	**5**	6	7	8	9	10	**11**	**12**	13	14	15	16	17	**18**	**19**	20	21	22	23	24	**25**	**26**	27	28	29	30

JUNE 2011

5
SUN
DIM.DOM.SON

Ascension Sunday   Ascensión

6
MON
LUN.LUN.MON

Bank Holiday (IR)
Queen's Birthday (NZ)
Foundation Day (WA - AU)

7
TUE
MAR.MAR.DIE

8
WED
MER.MIÉR.MIT

First Quarter ◑ 2:11 U.T.

9
THU
JEU.JUE.DON

10
FRI
VEN.VIER.FRE

11
SAT
SAM.SÁB.SAM

Queen's Official Birthday (tentative) (UK)

	F	S	S	M	T	W	TH	F	S	S	M	T	W	TH	F	S	S	M	T	W	TH	F	S	S	M	T	W	TH
MAY 2011		1	2	3	4	5	6	7	8	9	10	11	12	13	14	15	16	17	18	19	20	21	22	23	24	25	26	27	28	29	30	31
JUNE 2011					1	2	3	4	5	6	7	8	9	10	11	12	13	14	15	16	17	18	19	20	21	22	23	24	25	26	27	28	29	30
JULY 2011	1	2	3	4	5	6	7	8	9	10	11	12	13	14	15	16	17	18	19	20	21	22	23	24	25	26	27	28	29	30	31

12
SUN
DIM.DOM.SON

Pentecost (Whitsun)   Pentecôte   Pentecostés

13
MON
LUN.LUN.MON

Queen's Birthday (AU except WA)

Pentecost (Whit) Monday   Lundi de Pentecôte   Lunes de Pentecostés

14
TUE
MAR.MAR.DIE

Flag Day (US)

Full Moon ○ 20:14 U.T. / Lunar Eclipse (Total) 20:12 U.T.

15
WED
MER.MIÉR.MIT

16
THU
JEU.JUE.DON

17
FRI
VEN.VIER.FRE

18
SAT
SAM.SÁB.SAM

	F	S	S	M	T	W	TH	F	S	S	M	T	W	TH	F	S	S	M	T	W	TH	F	S	S	M	T	W	TH	F	S	S	M	T	W	TH
MAY 2011		1	2	3	4	5	6	7	8	9	10	11	12	13	14	15	16	17	18	19	20	21	22	23	24	25	26	27	28	29	30	31
JUNE 2011					1	2	3	4	5	6	7	8	9	10	11	12	13	14	15	16	17	18	19	20	21	22	23	24	25	26	27	28	29	30
JULY 2011	1	2	3	4	5	6	7	8	9	10	11	12	13	14	15	16	17	18	19	20	21	22	23	24	25	26	27	28	29	30	31

19
SUN
DIM.DOM.SON

Father's Day (US; CAN; UK)   Fête des Pères (CAN; FR)   Día del Padre (MX)

20
MON
LUN.LUN.MON

Summer Solstice 17:16 U.T.

21
TUE
MAR.MAR.DIE

National Aboriginal Day (CAN)

Journée internationale des populations autochtones (CAN)

22
WED
MER.MIÉR.MIT

Last Quarter ◑ 11:48 U.T.

23
THU
JEU.JUE.DON

24
FRI
VEN.VIER.FRE

Saint-Jean Baptiste (QC - CAN)

Fête nationale du Québec   Quebec National Day

25
SAT
SAM.SÁB.SAM

	F	S	S	M	T	W	TH	F	S	S	M	T	W	TH	F	S	S	M	T	W	TH	F	S	S	M	T	W	TH	F	S	S	M	T	W	TH
MAY 2011		1	2	3	4	5	6	7	8	9	10	11	12	13	14	15	16	17	18	19	20	21	22	23	24	25	26	27	28	29	30	31			
JUNE 2011					1	2	3	4	5	6	7	8	9	10	11	12	13	14	15	16	17	18	19	20	21	22	23	24	25	26	27	28	29	30	
JULY 2011	1	2	3	4	5	6	7	8	9	10	11	12	13	14	15	16	17	18	19	20	21	22	23	24	25	26	27	28	29	30	31				

26
SUN
DIM.DOM.SON

27
MON
LUN.LUN.MON

Discovery Day (NL - CAN)

28
TUE
MAR.MAR.DIE

29
WED
MER.MIÉR.MIT

30
THU
JEU.JUE.DON

JULY 2011

New Moon ● 9:54 U.T. / Solar Eclipse (Partial) 8:39 U.T.

1
FRI
VEN.VIER.FRE

Canada Day (CAN)　Fête du Canada (CAN)

2
SAT
SAM.SÁB.SAM

	F	S	S	M	T	W	TH	F	S	S	M	T	W	TH	F	S	S	M	T	W	TH	F	S	S	M	T	W	TH	F	S	S	M	T	W	TH
MAY 2011			1	2	3	4	5	6	**7**	**8**	9	10	11	12	13	**14**	**15**	16	17	18	19	20	**21**	**22**	23	24	25	26	27	**28**	**29**	30	31		
JUNE 2011					1	2	3	**4**	**5**	6	7	8	9	10	**11**	**12**	13	14	15	16	17	**18**	**19**	20	21	22	23	24	**25**	**26**	27	28	29	30	
JULY 2011	1	**2**	**3**	4	5	6	7	8	**9**	**10**	11	12	13	14	15	**16**	**17**	18	19	20	21	22	**23**	**24**	25	26	27	28	29	**30**	**31**				

3
SUN
DIM.DOM.SON

Aphelion 15:00 U.T.

4
MON
LUN.LUN.MON

Independence Day (US)

5
TUE
MAR.MAR.DIE

6
WED
MER.MIÉR.MIT

7
THU
JEU.JUE.DON

First Quarter ◐ 6:29 U.T.

8
FRI
VEN.VIER.FRE

9
SAT
SAM.SÁB.SAM

	F	S	S	M	T	W	TH	F	S	S	M	T	W	TH	F	S	S	M	T	W	TH	F	S	S	M	T	W	TH
JUNE 2011						1	2	3	4	5	6	7	8	9	10	11	12	13	14	15	16	17	18	19	20	21	22	23	24	25	26	27	28	29	30
JULY 2011	1	2	3	4	5	6	7	8	9	10	11	12	13	14	15	16	17	18	19	20	21	22	23	24	25	26	27	28	29	30	31
AUGUST 2011				1	2	3	4	5	6	7	8	9	10	11	12	13	14	15	16	17	18	19	20	21	22	23	24	25	26	27	28	29	30	31

10
SUN
DIM.DOM.SON

11
MON
LUN.LUN.MON

Feest van de Vlaamse Gemeenschap (BE)

12
TUE
MAR.MAR.DIE

Public Holiday (NIR)

13
WED
MER.MIÉR.MIT

14
THU
JEU.JUE.DON

Fête nationale de la France (FR)

Full Moon ○ 6:40 U.T.

15
FRI
VEN.VIER.FRE

16
SAT
SAM.SÁB.SAM

	F	S	S	M	T	W	TH	F	S	S	M	T	W	TH	F	S	S	M	T	W	TH	F	S	S	M	T	W	TH	F	S	S	M	T	W	TH
JUNE 2011					1	2	3	4	5	6	7	8	9	10	11	12	13	14	15	16	17	18	19	20	21	22	23	24	25	26	27	28	29	30	
JULY 2011	1	2	3	4	5	6	7	8	9	10	11	12	13	14	15	16	17	18	19	20	21	22	23	24	25	26	27	28	29	30	31				
AUGUST 2011				1	2	3	4	5	6	7	8	9	10	11	12	13	14	15	16	17	18	19	20	21	22	23	24	25	26	27	28	29	30	31	

17
SUN
DIM.DOM.SON

18
MON
LUN.LUN.MON

19
TUE
MAR.MAR.DIE

20
WED
MER.MIÉR.MIT

21
THU
JEU.JUE.DON

Nationale feestdag (BE)

Fête nationale de la Belgique (BE)

22
FRI
VEN.VIER.FRE

Last Quarter ◖ 5:02 U.T.

23
SAT
SAM.SÁB.SAM

		F	S	S	M	T	W	TH	F	S	S	M	T	W	TH	F	S	S	M	T	W	TH	F	S	S	M	T	W	TH
JUNE 2011							1	2	3	**4**	**5**	6	7	8	9	10	**11**	**12**	13	14	15	16	17	**18**	**19**	20	21	22	23	24	**25**	**26**	27	28	29	30
JULY 2011	1	**2**	**3**	4	5	6	7	8	**9**	**10**	11	12	13	14	15	**16**	**17**	18	19	20	21	22	**23**	**24**	25	26	27	28	29	**30**	**31**
AUGUST 2011			1	2	3	4	5	**6**	**7**	8	9	10	11	12	**13**	**14**	15	16	17	18	19	**20**	**21**	22	23	24	25	26	**27**	**28**	29	30	31

24
SUN
DIM.DOM.SON

25
MON
LUN.LUN.MON

26
TUE
MAR.MAR.DIE

27
WED
MER.MIÉR.MIT

28
THU
JEU.JUE.DON

29
FRI
VEN.VIER.FRE

New Moon ● 18:40 U

30
SAT
SAM.SÁB.SAM

	F	S	S	M	T	W	TH	F	S	S	M	T	W	TH	F	S	S	M	T	W	TH	F	S	S	M	T	W	TH	F	S	S	M	T	W	TH
JUNE 2011						1	2	3	**4**	**5**	6	7	8	9	10	**11**	**12**	13	14	15	16	17	**18**	**19**	20	21	22	23	24	**25**	**26**	27	28	29	30
JULY 2011	1	**2**	**3**	4	5	6	7	8	**9**	**10**	11	12	13	14	15	**16**	**17**	18	19	20	21	22	**23**	**24**	25	26	27	28	29	**30**	**31**				
AUGUST 2011				1	2	3	4	5	**6**	**7**	8	9	10	11	12	**13**	**14**	15	16	17	18	19	**20**	**21**	22	23	24	25	26	**27**	**28**	29	30	31	

31
SUN
DIM.DOM.SON

Ramadan begins at sundown

AUGUST 2011

1
MON
LUN.LUN.MON

Picnic Day (NT - AU)

Bank Holiday (IR; SCT)

Civic Holiday (CAN)   Congé civique (CAN)

2
TUE
MAR.MAR.DIE

3
WED
MER.MIÉR.MIT

4
THU
JEU.JUE.DON

5
FRI
VEN.VIER.FRE

First Quarter ◑ 11:08 U.T.

6
SAT
SAM.SÁB.SAM

		TH	F	S	S	M	T	W	TH	F	S	S	M	T	W	TH	F	S	S	M	T	W	TH	F	S	S	M	T	W	TH	F	S	S	M	T	W
JULY 2011			1	2	3	4	5	6	7	8	9	10	11	12	13	14	15	16	17	18	19	20	21	22	23	24	25	26	27	28	29	30	31			
AUGUST 2011						1	2	3	4	5	6	7	8	9	10	11	12	13	14	15	16	17	18	19	20	21	22	23	24	25	26	27	28	29	30	31
SEPTEMBER 2011	1	2	3	4	5	6	7	8	9	10	11	12	13	14	15	16	17	18	19	20	21	22	23	24	25	26	27	28	29	30						

7
SUN
DIM.DOM.SON

8
MON
LUN.LUN.MON

9
TUE
MAR.MAR.DIE

10
WED
MER.MIÉR.MIT

11
THU
JEU.JUE.DON

12
FRI
VEN.VIER.FRE

Full Moon ◯ 18:57 U.

13
SAT
SAM.SÁB.SAM

	TH	F	S	S	M	T	W	TH	F	S	S	M	T	W	TH	F	S	S	M	T	W	TH	F	S	S	M	T	W	TH	F	S	S	M	T	W
JULY 2011		1	2	3	4	5	6	7	8	9	10	11	12	13	14	15	16	17	18	19	20	21	22	23	24	25	26	27	28	29	30	31			
AUGUST 2011					1	2	3	4	5	6	7	8	9	10	11	12	13	14	15	16	17	18	19	20	21	22	23	24	25	26	27	28	29	30	31
SEPTEMBER 2011	1	2	3	4	5	6	7	8	9	10	11	12	13	14	15	16	17	18	19	20	21	22	23	24	25	26	27	28	29	30					

14
SUN
DIM.DOM.SON

15
MON
LUN.LUN.MON

Discovery Day (YT - CAN)

Assumption   Assomption   Asunción de María

16
TUE
MAR.MAR.DIE

17
WED
MER.MIÉR.MIT

18
THU
JEU.JUE.DON

19
FRI
VEN.VIER.FRE

20
SAT
SAM.SÁB.SAM

	TH	F	S	S	M	T	W	TH	F	S	S	M	T	W	TH	F	S	S	M	T	W	TH	F	S	S	M	T	W	TH	F	S	S	M	T	W
JULY 2011		1	2	3	4	5	6	7	8	9	10	11	12	13	14	15	16	17	18	19	20	21	22	23	24	25	26	27	28	29	30	31			
AUGUST 2011					1	2	3	4	5	6	7	8	9	10	11	12	13	14	15	16	17	18	19	20	21	22	23	24	25	26	27	28	29	30	31
SEPTEMBER 2011	1	2	3	4	5	6	7	8	9	10	11	12	13	14	15	16	17	18	19	20	21	22	23	24	25	26	27	28	29	30					

Last Quarter ◑ 21:54 U.T

21
SUN
DIM.DOM.SON

22
MON
LUN.LUN.MON

23
TUE
MAR.MAR.DIE

24
WED
MER.MIÉR.MIT

25
THU
JEU.JUE.DON

26
FRI
VEN.VIER.FRE

27
SAT
SAM.SÁB.SAM

	TH	F	S	S	M	T	W	TH	F	S	S	M	T	W	TH	F	S	S	M	T	W	TH	F	S	S	M	T	W	TH	F	S	S	M	T	W
JULY 2011		1	2	3	4	5	6	7	8	9	10	11	12	13	14	15	16	17	18	19	20	21	22	23	24	25	26	27	28	29	30	31			
AUGUST 2011			1	2	3	4	5	6	7	8	9	10	11	12	13	14	15	16	17	18	19	20	21	22	23	24	25	26	27	28	29	30	31		
SEPTEMBER 2011	1	2	3	4	5	6	7	8	9	10	11	12	13	14	15	16	17	18	19	20	21	22	23	24	25	26	27	28	29	30					

28
SUN
DIM.DOM.SON

New Moon ● 3:04 U.T.

29
MON
LUN.LUN.MON

Eid-al-Fitr begins at sundown

Summer Bank Holiday (ENG, WAL, NIR)

30
TUE
MAR.MAR.DIE

31
WED
MER.MIÉR.MIT

SEPTEMBER2011

1
THU
JEU.JUE.DON

2
FRI
VEN.VIER.FRE

3
SAT
SAM.SÁB.SAM

	TH	F	S	S	M	T	W	TH	F	S	S	M	T	W	TH	F	S	S	M	T	W	TH	F	S	S	M	T	W	TH	F	S	S	M	T	W
JULY 2011		1	2	3	4	5	6	7	8	9	10	11	12	13	14	15	16	17	18	19	20	21	22	23	24	25	26	27	28	29	30	31			
AUGUST 2011					1	2	3	4	5	6	7	8	9	10	11	12	13	14	15	16	17	18	19	20	21	22	23	24	25	26	27	28	29	30	31
SEPTEMBER 2011	1	2	3	4	5	6	7	8	9	10	11	12	13	14	15	16	17	18	19	20	21	22	23	24	25	26	27	28	29	30					

First Quarter ◗ 17:39 U.T.

4
SUN
DIM.DOM.SON

Father's Day (AU; NZ)

5
MON
LUN.LUN.MON

Labor Day (US)

Labour Day (CAN)   Fête du Travail (CAN)

6
TUE
MAR.MAR.DIE

7
WED
MER.MIÉR.MIT

8
THU
JEU.JUE.DON

9
FRI
VEN.VIER.FRE

10
SAT
SAM.SÁB.SAM

	TH	F	S	S	M	T	W	TH	F	S	S	M	T	W	TH	F	S	S	M	T	W	TH	F	S	S	M	T	W	TH	F	S	S	M	T	W
AUGUST 2011					1	2	3	4	5	6	7	8	9	10	11	12	13	14	15	16	17	18	19	20	21	22	23	24	25	26	27	28	29	30	31
SEPTEMBER 2011	1	2	3	4	5	6	7	8	9	10	11	12	13	14	15	16	17	18	19	20	21	22	23	24	25	26	27	28	29	30					
OCTOBER 2011			1	2	3	4	5	6	7	8	9	10	11	12	13	14	15	16	17	18	19	20	21	22	23	24	25	26	27	28	29	30	31		

11
SUN
DIM.DOM.SON

9/11 Remembrance

Full Moon ◯ 9:27 U.T.

12
MON
LUN.LUN.MON

13
TUE
MAR.MAR.DIE

14
WED
MER.MIÉR.MIT

15
THU
JEU.JUE.DON

Noche del Grito (MX)

16
FRI
VEN.VIER.FRE

Día de la Independencia (MX)

17
SAT
SAM.SÁB.SAM

		TH	F	S	S	M	T	W	TH	F	S	S	M	T	W	TH	F	S	S	M	T	W	TH	F	S	S	M	T	W	TH	F	S	S	M	T	W
AUGUST 2011						1	2	3	4	5	6	7	8	9	10	11	12	13	14	15	16	17	18	19	20	21	22	23	24	25	26	27	28	29	30	31
SEPTEMBER 2011	1	2	3	4	5	6	7	8	9	10	11	12	13	14	15	16	17	18	19	20	21	22	23	24	25	26	27	28	29	30						
OCTOBER 2011		1	2	3	4	5	6	7	8	9	10	11	12	13	14	15	16	17	18	19	20	21	22	23	24	25	26	27	28	29	30	31				

18
SUN
DIM.DOM.SON

19
MON
LUN.LUN.MON

Last Quarter ◑ 13:39 U.

20
TUE
MAR.MAR.DIE

21
WED
MER.MIÉR.MIT

UN International Day of Peac

22
THU
JEU.JUE.DON

Autumnal Equinox 9:04 U.

23
FRI
VEN.VIER.FRE

24
SAT
SAM.SÁB.SAM

	TH	F	S	S	M	T	W	TH	F	S	S	M	T	W	TH	F	S	S	M	T	W	TH	F	S	S	M	T	W	TH	F	S	S	M	T	W
AUGUST 2011					1	2	3	4	5	**6**	**7**	8	9	10	11	12	**13**	**14**	15	16	17	18	19	**20**	**21**	22	23	24	25	26	**27**	**28**	29	30	31
SEPTEMBER 2011	1	2	**3**	**4**	5	6	7	8	9	**10**	**11**	12	13	14	15	16	**17**	**18**	19	20	21	22	23	**24**	**25**	26	27	28	29	30					
OCTOBER 2011			**1**	**2**	3	4	5	6	7	**8**	**9**	10	11	12	13	14	**15**	**16**	17	18	19	20	21	**22**	**23**	24	25	26	27	28	**29**	**30**	31		

25
SUN
DIM.DOM.SON

Daylight Saving Time begins (NZ)

26
MON
LUN.LUN.MON

New Moon ● 11:09 U.T.

27
TUE
MAR.MAR.DIE

Fête de la Communauté française (BE)

28
WED
MER.MIÉR.MIT

Rosh Hashanah begins at sundown

29
THU
JEU.JUE.DON

30
FRI
VEN.VIER.FRE

OCTOBER 2011

1
SAT
SAM.SÁB.SAM

	TH	F	S	S	M	T	W	TH	F	S	S	M	T	W	TH	F	S	S	M	T	W	TH	F	S	S	M	T	W
AUGUST 2011					1	2	3	4	5	**6**	**7**	8	9	10	11	12	**13**	**14**	15	16	17	18	19	**20**	**21**	22	23	24	25	26	**27**	**28**	29	30	31
SEPTEMBER 2011	1	2	**3**	**4**	5	6	7	8	9	**10**	**11**	12	13	14	15	16	**17**	**18**	19	20	21	22	23	**24**	**25**	26	27	28	29	30
OCTOBER 2011		**1**	**2**	3	4	5	6	7	**8**	**9**	10	11	12	13	14	**15**	**16**	17	18	19	20	21	**22**	**23**	24	25	26	27	28	**29**	**30**	31

OCTOBER 2011
OCTOBRE · OCTUBRE · OKTOBER

2
SUN
DIM.DOM.SON

3
MON
LUN.LUN.MON

Labour Day (NSW, SA - AU

Queen's Birthday (WA - AU

First Quarter ◗ 3:15 U.T

4
TUE
MAR.MAR.DIE

World Animal Day

5
WED
MER.MIÉR.MIT

6
THU
JEU.JUE.DON

7
FRI
VEN.VIER.FRE

Yom Kippur begins at sundown

8
SAT
SAM.SÁB.SAM

	TH	F	S	S	M	T	W	TH	F	S	S	M	T	W	TH	F	S	S	M	T	W	TH	F	S	S	M	T	W
SEPTEMBER 2011	1	2	3	4	5	6	7	8	9	10	11	12	13	14	15	16	17	18	19	20	21	22	23	24	25	26	27	28	29	30
OCTOBER 2011			1	2	3	4	5	6	7	8	9	10	11	12	13	14	15	16	17	18	19	20	21	22	23	24	25	26	27	28	29	30	31
NOVEMBER 2011					1	2	3	4	5	6	7	8	9	10	11	12	13	14	15	16	17	18	19	20	21	22	23	24	25	26	27	28	29	30

9
SUN
DIM.DOM.SON

10
MON
LUN.LUN.MON

Columbus Day (US)

Thanksgiving Day (CAN)   Action de grâce (CAN)

11
TUE
MAR.MAR.DIE

Full Moon ◯ 2:06 U.T.

12
WED
MER.MIÉR.MIT

Día de la Raza (MX)

13
THU
JEU.JUE.DON

14
FRI
VEN.VIER.FRE

15
SAT
SAM.SÁB.SAM

		TH	F	S	S	M	T	W	TH	F	S	S	M	T	W	TH	F	S	S	M	T	W	TH	F	S	S	M	T	W	TH	F	S	S	M	T	W
SEPTEMBER 2011		1	2	3	4	5	6	7	8	9	10	11	12	13	14	15	16	17	18	19	20	21	22	23	24	25	26	27	28	29	30					
OCTOBER 2011			1	2	3	4	5	6	7	8	9	10	11	12	13	14	15	16	17	18	19	20	21	22	23	24	25	26	27	28	29	30	31			
NOVEMBER 2011				1	2	3	4	5	6	7	8	9	10	11	12	13	14	15	16	17	18	19	20	21	22	23	24	25	26	27	28	29	30		

16
SUN
DIM.DOM.SON

17
MON
LUN.LUN.MON

18
TUE
MAR.MAR.DIE

19
WED
MER.MIÉR.MIT

Last Quarter ◑ 3:30 U.T.

20
THU
JEU.JUE.DON

21
FRI
VEN.VIER.FRE

22
SAT
SAM.SÁB.SAM

	TH	F	S	S	M	T	W	TH	F	S	S	M	T	W	TH	F	S	S	M	T	W	TH	F	S	S	M	T	W	TH	F	S	S	M	T	W
SEPTEMBER 2011	1	2	3	4	5	6	7	8	9	10	11	12	13	14	15	16	17	18	19	20	21	22	23	24	25	26	27	28	29	30					
OCTOBER 2011			1	2	3	4	5	6	7	8	9	10	11	12	13	14	15	16	17	18	19	20	21	22	23	24	25	26	27	28	29	30	31		
NOVEMBER 2011					1	2	3	4	5	6	7	8	9	10	11	12	13	14	15	16	17	18	19	20	21	22	23	24	25	26	27	28	29	30	

23
SUN
DIM.DOM.SON

Labour Day (NZ)

United Nations Day

24
MON
LUN.LUN.MON

25
TUE
MAR.MAR.DIE

New Moon ● 19:56 U.T.

26
WED
MER.MIÉR.MIT

27
THU
JEU.JUE.DON

28
FRI
VEN.VIER.FRE

29
SAT
SAM.SÁB.SAM

		TH	F	S	S	M	T	W	TH	F	S	S	M	T	W	TH	F	S	S	M	T	W	TH	F	S	S	M	T	W	TH	F	S	S	M	T	W
SEPTEMBER 2011		1	2	**3**	**4**	5	6	7	8	9	**10**	**11**	12	13	14	15	16	**17**	**18**	19	20	21	22	23	**24**	**25**	26	27	28	29	30					
OCTOBER 2011				**1**	**2**	3	4	5	6	7	**8**	**9**	10	11	12	13	14	**15**	**16**	17	18	19	20	21	**22**	**23**	24	25	26	27	28	**29**	**30**	31		
NOVEMBER 2011						1	2	3	4	**5**	**6**	7	8	9	10	11	**12**	**13**	14	15	16	17	18	**19**	**20**	21	22	23	24	25	**26**	**27**	28	29	30	

OCTOBER 2011

30
SUN
DIM.DOM.SON

European Union Daylight Saving Time ends

31
MON
LUN.LUN.MON

Halloween

Bank Holiday (IR)

NOVEMBER 2011

1
TUE
MAR.MAR.DIE

Melbourne Cup (AU)

All Saints' Day   Toussaint   Día de Todos los Santos

First Quarter ◑ 16:38 U.T

2
WED
MER.MIÉR.MIT

All Souls' Day

Día de los Muertos (MX

3
THU
JEU.JUE.DON

4
FRI
VEN.VIER.FRE

5
SAT
SAM.SÁB.SAM

Bonfire Night (UK)

Eid al-Adha begins at sundown

	TH	F	S	S	M	T	W	TH	F	S	S	M	T	W	TH	F	S	S	M	T	W	TH	F	S	S	M	T	W	TH	F	S	S	M	T	W
OCTOBER 2011			**1**	**2**	3	4	5	6	7	**8**	**9**	10	11	12	13	14	**15**	**16**	17	18	19	20	21	**22**	**23**	24	25	26	27	28	**29**	**30**	31		
NOVEMBER 2011					1	2	3	4	**5**	**6**	7	8	9	10	11	**12**	**13**	14	15	16	17	18	**19**	**20**	21	22	23	24	25	**26**	**27**	28	29	30	
DECEMBER 2011	1	2	**3**	**4**	5	6	7	8	9	**10**	**11**	12	13	14	15	16	**17**	**18**	19	20	21	22	23	**24**	**25**	26	27	28	29	30	**31**				

©2010 Carol Simow

6
SUN
DIM.DOM.SON

Daylight Saving Time ends (US; CAN)

7
MON
LUN.LUN.MON

8
TUE
MAR.MAR.DIE

Election Day (US)

9
WED
MER.MIÉR.MIT

Full Moon ○ 20:16 U.T.

10
THU
JEU.JUE.DON

11
FRI
VEN.VIER.FRE

Veterans' Day (US)

Remembrance Day (AU; CAN)   Jour du Souvenir (CAN)

Armistice (FR)

12
SAT
SAM.SÁB.SAM

		TH	F	S	S	M	T	W	TH	F	S	S	M	T	W	TH	F	S	S	M	T	W	TH	F	S	S	M	T	W	TH	F	S	S	M	T	W
OCTOBER 2011				**1**	**2**	3	4	5	6	7	**8**	**9**	10	11	12	13	14	**15**	**16**	17	18	19	20	21	**22**	**23**	24	25	26	27	28	**29**	**30**	31		
NOVEMBER 2011							1	2	3	4	**5**	**6**	7	8	9	10	11	**12**	**13**	14	15	16	17	18	**19**	**20**	21	22	23	24	25	**26**	**27**	28	29	30
DECEMBER 2011	1	2	**3**	**4**	5	6	7	8	9	**10**	**11**	12	13	14	15	16	**17**	**18**	19	20	21	22	23	**24**	**25**	26	27	28	29	30	**31**				

13
SUN
DIM.DOM.SON

Remembrance Sunday (UK)

14
MON
LUN.LUN.MON

15
TUE
MAR.MAR.DIE

Koningsdag (BE)

Fête du Roi (BE)

16
WED
MER.MIÉR.MIT

17
THU
JEU.JUE.DON

18
FRI
VEN.VIER.FRE

Last Quarter ◑ 15:09 U.T.

19
SAT
SAM.SÁB.SAM

	TH	F	S	S	M	T	W	TH	F	S	S	M	T	W	TH	F	S	S	M	T	W	TH	F	S	S	M	T	W	TH	F	S	S	M	T	W
OCTOBER 2011			1	2	3	4	5	6	7	8	9	10	11	12	13	14	15	16	17	18	19	20	21	22	23	24	25	26	27	28	29	30	31		
NOVEMBER 2011						1	2	3	4	5	6	7	8	9	10	11	12	13	14	15	16	17	18	19	20	21	22	23	24	25	26	27	28	29	30
DECEMBER 2011	1	2	3	4	5	6	7	8	9	10	11	12	13	14	15	16	17	18	19	20	21	22	23	24	25	26	27	28	29	30	31				

20
SUN
DIM.DOM.SON

Día de la Revolución Mexicana (MX)

21
MON
LUN.LUN.MON

22
TUE
MAR.MAR.DIE

23
WED
MER.MIÉR.MIT

24
THU
JEU.JUE.DON

Thanksgiving Day (US)

New Moon ● 6:10 U.T. / Solar Eclipse (Partial) 6:21 U.T.

25
FRI
VEN.VIER.FRE

26
SAT
SAM.SÁB.SAM

	TH	F	S	S	M	T	W	TH	F	S	S	M	T	W	TH	F	S	S	M	T	W	TH	F	S	S	M	T	W	TH	F	S	S	M	T	W
OCTOBER 2011			**1**	**2**	3	4	5	6	7	**8**	**9**	10	11	12	13	14	**15**	**16**	17	18	19	20	21	**22**	**23**	24	25	26	27	28	**29**	**30**	31		
NOVEMBER 2011					1	2	3	4	**5**	**6**	7	8	9	10	11	**12**	**13**	14	15	16	17	18	**19**	**20**	21	22	23	24	25	**26**	**27**	28	29	30	
DECEMBER 2011	1	2	**3**	**4**	5	6	7	8	9	**10**	**11**	12	13	14	15	16	**17**	**18**	19	20	21	22	23	**24**	**25**	26	27	28	29	30	**31**				

27
SUN
DIM.DOM.SON

Advent   Avent   Adviento

28
MON
LUN.LUN.MON

29
TUE
MAR.MAR.DIE

30
WED
MER.MIÉR.MIT

St. Andrew's Day (SCT)

DECEMBER 2011

1
THU
JEU.JUE.DON

First Quarter ◑ 9:52 U.T.

2
FRI
VEN.VIER.FRE

3
SAT
SAM.SÁB.SAM

	TH	F	S	S	M	T	W	TH	F	S	S	M	T	W	TH	F	S	S	M	T	W	TH	F	S	S	M	T	W	TH	F	S	S	M	T	W
NOVEMBER 2011						1	2	3	4	5	6	7	8	9	10	11	12	13	14	15	16	17	18	19	20	21	22	23	24	25	26	27	28	29	30
DECEMBER 2011	1	2	3	4	5	6	7	8	9	10	11	12	13	14	15	16	17	18	19	20	21	22	23	24	25	26	27	28	29	30	31				
JANUARY 2012			1	2	3	4	5	6	7	8	9	10	11	12	13	14	15	16	17	18	19	20	21	22	23	24	25	26	27	28	29	30	31		

4
SUN
DIM.DOM.SON

5
MON
LUN.LUN.MON

6
TUE
MAR.MAR.DIE

nterklaas (BE)

aint-Nicolas (BE)

7
WED
MER.MIÉR.MIT

arl Harbor Remembrance

8
THU
JEU.JUE.DON

9
FRI
VEN.VIER.FRE

ll Moon ◯ 14:36 U.T. / Lunar Eclipse (Total) 14:36 U.T.

10
SAT
SAM.SÁB.SAM

	TH	F	S	S	M	T	W	TH	F	S	S	M	T	W	TH	F	S	S	M	T	W	TH	F	S	S	M	T	W	TH	F	S	S	M	T	W
NOVEMBER 2011						1	2	3	4	5	6	7	8	9	10	11	12	13	14	15	16	17	18	19	20	21	22	23	24	25	26	27	28	29	30
DECEMBER 2011	1	2	3	4	5	6	7	8	9	10	11	12	13	14	15	16	17	18	19	20	21	22	23	24	25	26	27	28	29	30	31				
JANUARY 2012			1	2	3	4	5	6	7	8	9	10	11	12	13	14	15	16	17	18	19	20	21	22	23	24	25	26	27	28	29	30	31		

11
SUN
DIM.DOM.SON

12
MON
LUN.LUN.MON

Día de la Virgen de Guadalupe (MX)

13
TUE
MAR.MAR.DIE

14
WED
MER.MIÉR.MIT

15
THU
JEU.JUE.DON

16
FRI
VEN.VIER.FRE

Las Posadas (M

17
SAT
SAM.SÁB.SAM

	TH	F	S	S	M	T	W	TH	F	S	S	M	T	W	TH	F	S	S	M	T	W	TH	F	S	S	M	T	W
NOVEMBER 2011						1	2	3	4	5	6	7	8	9	10	11	12	13	14	15	16	17	18	19	20	21	22	23	24	25	26	27	28	29	30
DECEMBER 2011	1	2	3	4	5	6	7	8	9	10	11	12	13	14	15	16	17	18	19	20	21	22	23	24	25	26	27	28	29	30	31
JANUARY 2012			1	2	3	4	5	6	7	8	9	10	11	12	13	14	15	16	17	18	19	20	21	22	23	24	25	26	27	28	29	30	31

Last Quarter ◑ 0:48 U.T.

18
SUN
DIM.DOM.SON

19
MON
LUN.LUN.MON

20
TUE
MAR.MAR.DIE

Hanukkah begins at sundown

21
WED
MER.MIÉR.MIT

Winter Solstice 5:30 U.T.

22
THU
JEU.JUE.DON

23
FRI
VEN.VIER.FRE

New Moon ● 18:06 U.T.

24
SAT
SAM.SÁB.SAM

Christmas Eve   Veille de Noël   Noche Buena

	TH	F	S	S	M	T	W	TH	F	S	S	M	T	W	TH	F	S	S	M	T	W	TH	F	S	S	M	T	W
NOVEMBER 2011						1	2	3	4	5	6	7	8	9	10	11	12	13	14	15	16	17	18	19	20	21	22	23	24	25	26	27	28	29	30
DECEMBER 2011	1	2	3	4	5	6	7	8	9	10	11	12	13	14	15	16	17	18	19	20	21	22	23	24	25	26	27	28	29	30	31
JANUARY 2012			1	2	3	4	5	6	7	8	9	10	11	12	13	14	15	16	17	18	19	20	21	22	23	24	25	26	27	28	29	30	31

25
SUN
DIM.DOM.SON

Christmas Day   Noël   Navida

26
MON
LUN.LUN.MON

Kwanzaa begin
St. Stephen's Day (IR; LU
Bank Holiday (UK

27
TUE
MAR.MAR.DIE

Boxing Da
L'après-Noël (CAN

28
WED
MER.MIÉR.MIT

Proclamation Day (SA - AU

29
THU
JEU.JUE.DON

30
FRI
VEN.VIER.FRE

31
SAT
SAM.SÁB.SAM

New Year's Eve   Saint-Sylvestre   Fin de Añ

	TH	F	S	S	M	T	W	TH	F	S	S	M	T	W	TH	F	S	S	M	T	W	TH	F	S	S	M	T	W
NOVEMBER 2011						1	2	3	4	5	6	7	8	9	10	11	12	13	14	15	16	17	18	19	20	21	22	23 24 25 26 27 28 29 30
DECEMBER 2011	1	2	3	4	5	6	7	8	9	10	11	12	13	14	15	16	17	18	19	20	21	22	23	24	25	26	27	28 29 30 31
JANUARY 2012			1	2	3	4	5	6	7	8	9	10	11	12	13	14	15	16	17	18	19	20	21	22	23	24	25	26 27 28 29 30 31

©2010 Isabelle Francais

2012 YEAR PLANNER

JANUARY	FEBRUARY	MARCH	APRIL
1 SUN	1 WED	1 THU	1 SUN
2 MON	2 THU	2 FRI	2 MON
3 TUE	3 FRI	3 SAT	3 TUE
4 WED	4 SAT	4 SUN	4 WED
5 THU	5 SUN	5 MON	5 THU
6 FRI	6 MON	6 TUE	6 FRI
7 SAT	7 TUE	7 WED	7 SAT
8 SUN	8 WED	8 THU	8 SUN
9 MON	9 THU	9 FRI	9 MON
10 TUE	10 FRI	10 SAT	10 TUE
11 WED	11 SAT	11 SUN	11 WED
12 THU	12 SUN	12 MON	12 THU
13 FRI	13 MON	13 TUE	13 FRI
14 SAT	14 TUE	14 WED	14 SAT
15 SUN	15 WED	15 THU	15 SUN
16 MON	16 THU	16 FRI	16 MON
17 TUE	17 FRI	17 SAT	17 TUE
18 WED	18 SAT	18 SUN	18 WED
19 THU	19 SUN	19 MON	19 THU
20 FRI	20 MON	20 TUE	20 FRI
21 SAT	21 TUE	21 WED	21 SAT
22 SUN	22 WED	22 THU	22 SUN
23 MON	23 THU	23 FRI	23 MON
24 TUE	24 FRI	24 SAT	24 TUE
25 WED	25 SAT	25 SUN	25 WED
26 THU	26 SUN	26 MON	26 THU
27 FRI	27 MON	27 TUE	27 FRI
28 SAT	28 TUES	28 WED	28 SAT
29 SUN	29 WED	29 THU	29 SUN
30 MON		30 FRI	30 MON
31 TUES		31 SAT	

2012 YEAR PLANNER

MAY	JUNE	JULY	AUGUST
1 TUE	1 FRI	**1 SUN**	1 WED
2 WED	**2 SAT**	2 MON	2 THU
3 THU	**3 SUN**	3 TUE	3 FRI
4 FRI	4 MON	4 WED	**4 SAT**
5 SAT	5 TUE	5 THU	**5 SUN**
6 SUN	6 WED	6 FRI	6 MON
7 MON	7 THU	**7 SAT**	7 TUE
8 TUE	8 FRI	**8 SUN**	8 WED
9 WED	**9 SAT**	9 MON	9 THU
10 THU	**10 SUN**	10 TUE	10 FRI
11 FRI	11 MON	11 WED	**11 SAT**
12 SAT	12 TUE	12 THU	**12 SUN**
13 SUN	13 WED	13 FRI	13 MON
14 MON	14 THU	**14 SAT**	14 TUE
15 TUE	15 FRI	**15 SUN**	15 WED
16 WED	**16 SAT**	16 MON	16 THU
17 THU	**17 SUN**	17 TUE	17 FRI
18 FRI	18 MON	18 WED	**18 SAT**
19 SAT	19 TUE	19 THU	**19 SUN**
20 SUN	20 WED	20 FRI	20 MON
21 MON	21 THU	**21 SAT**	21 TUE
22 TUE	22 FRI	**22 SUN**	22 WED
23 WED	**23 SAT**	23 MON	23 THU
24 THU	**24 SUN**	24 TUE	24 FRI
25 FRI	25 MON	25 WED	**25 SAT**
26 SAT	26 TUE	26 THU	**26 SUN**
27 SUN	27 WED	27 FRI	27 MON
28 MON	28 THU	**28 SAT**	28 TUE
29 TUE	29 FRI	**29 SUN**	29 WED
30 WED	**30 SAT**	30 MON	30 THU
31 THU		31 TUE	31 FRI

2012 YEAR PLANNER

SEPTEMBER	OCTOBER	NOVEMBER	DECEMBER
1 SAT	1 MON	1 THU	1 SAT
2 SUN	2 TUE	2 FRI	2 SUN
3 MON	3 WED	3 SAT	3 MON
4 TUE	4 THU	4 SUN	4 TUE
5 WED	5 FRI	5 MON	5 WED
6 THU	6 SAT	6 TUE	6 THU
7 FRI	7 SUN	7 WED	7 FRI
8 SAT	8 MON	8 THU	8 SAT
9 SUN	9 TUE	9 FRI	9 SUN
10 MON	10 WED	10 SAT	10 MON
11 TUE	11 THU	11 SUN	11 TUE
12 WED	12 FRI	12 MON	12 WED
13 THU	13 SAT	13 TUE	13 THU
14 FRI	14 SUN	14 WED	14 FRI
15 SAT	15 MON	15 THU	15 SAT
16 SUN	16 TUE	16 FRI	16 SUN
17 MON	17 WED	17 SAT	17 MON
18 TUE	18 THU	18 SUN	18 TUE
19 WED	19 FRI	19 MON	19 WED
20 THU	20 SAT	20 TUE	20 THU
21 FRI	21 SUN	21 WED	21 FRI
22 SAT	22 MON	22 THU	22 SAT
23 SUN	23 TUE	23 FRI	23 SUN
24 MON	24 WED	24 SAT	24 MON
25 TUE	25 THU	25 SUN	25 TUE
26 WED	26 FRI	26 MON	26 WED
27 THU	27 SAT	27 TUE	27 THU
28 FRI	28 SUN	28 WED	28 FRI
29 SAT	29 MON	29 THU	29 SAT
30 SUN	30 TUES	30 FRI	30 SUN
	31 WED		31 MON

NOTES

NOTES

NOTES

NOTES

NOTES

NOTES

NOTES

NOTES

NOTES